DATE DUE

JE 5 '94			
OC 10 97			
AP 13 00			

DEMCO 38-296

Understanding the Anasazi of
Mesa Verde
and Hovenweep

Cliff Palace. Photo by David Noble

Understanding the Anasazi of
Mesa Verde
and Hovenweep

Edited by

David Grant Noble

Cliff Palace. Lithograph by Eugene Kingman.

Ancient City Press
Santa Fe, New Mexico

Cover photo: Cliff Palace 1991 by David Grant Noble.
Courtesy of the photographer.

Back cover photo: Navajo Canyon, Mesa Verde. Lithograph by Eugene
Kingman. Courtesy Kingman daughters.

International Standard Book Number: 0-941270-71-8

Assistant editor: Melinda Elliott

Design and photo research: Deborah Flynn

First Ancient City Press edition.

Originally published in 1985 by the School of American Research.

10 9 8 7 6 5 4 3 2 1

Contents

North rim of the Mesa Verde looking toward Ute Mountain, 1985. Photo by Paul Logsdon.

PREHISTORIC DEVELOPMENTS
in the Mesa Verde Region

By Arthur H. Rohn

Mesa Verde is one of the best-known and certainly one of the most beautiful archaeological areas of the American Southwest. Not only have its sheer cliffs and deep canyons sheltered many prehistoric dwellings from the ravages of erosion, but the mesa top is virtually blanketed with the remains of ancient sites. However, after decades of public attention focused on this extraordinary national park, we are finding that Mesa Verde represents only a portion of a larger prehistoric cultural region.

During the Anasazi, or late prehistoric occupation of the Four Corners country, those lands lying north of the San Juan River formed a northern frontier of Pueblo culture. This northern San Juan region ranges from the Abajo Mountains and Comb Ridge in southeastern Utah through the Montezuma Valley, Mesa Verde, and valleys of the Mancos, La Plata, Animas, Piedra, and Pine rivers, to the Upper San Juan River Valley near Pagosa Springs, Colorado. The limits of Pueblo occupation at times encompassed only a portion of this area, though at other times Mesa Verde people could be found as far west as the Colorado River. It was within this entire region that the Mesa Verde style of Pueblo culture developed.

The best-known archaeological investigations have been conducted on the Mesa Verde itself, although we now know that it was only a part of a larger regional system centered in the adjacent Montezuma Valley. This valley northwest of the Mesa Verde is drained by many nonpermanent streams, and it provided ample land for prehistoric settlers. A number of large sites have been identified in this valley in recent years, including Yellow Jacket, Lowry Ruins, Yucca House, Mud Springs Ruin, Wilson Ruin, and others. An understanding of these prehistoric communities makes our knowledge of Mesa Verde more intelligible.

Archaeological sites have been found all over the Mesa Verde's many finger mesas and canyons, and definite population concentrations have been recognized, especially on Chapin and Wetherill mesas. Chapin mesa is the portion of the Mesa Verde that has been visited by the public for more than seventy-five years, and boasts many of the most famous ruins— Cliff Palace, Spruce Tree House, Balcony House, Far View House, Sun Temple, and Cedar Tree Tower. Another dozen sites, including Long House and Mug House, have been investigated on Wetherill Mesa. Today, our accumulated store of archaeological data about Mesa Verde, combined with our growing knowledge of the nearby Montezuma Valley, allows us to trace the developmental history of the entire region with its many interrelated communities.

THE BASKETMAKERS

Prior to about A.D. 575, traces of Anasazi or pre-Anasazi human occupation in this area are very scarce. Scattered stone projectile points, probably the tips for darts propelled by throwing boards, or *atlatls*, have turned up consistently on the Mesa Verde even though the campsites of these early inhabitants have yet to be found. The most ancient points are dated between 3000 and 1000 B.C., and later ones 700 B.C. to A.D. 450, the earliest Anasazi stage. These early peoples apparently hunted on the Mesa Verde and camped wherever they found themselves at the end of the day. Traces of their brief stay, such as their campfires and chips of stone made while repairing their tools, may have been covered up gradually by activities of the later dense occupations.

By A.D. 600, Anasazi settlers, called Basketmakers, had established a village of eight pithouses near Twin Trees on Chapin Mesa. Although only two of these houses, one of which is called Earth Lodge B, have been excavated, we can guess from recent work in similar villages near Yellow Jacket in the Montezuma Valley that this village also contained outdoor storage rooms and covered work spaces.

These Basketmaker people had become sedentary farmers who raised corn, beans, and squash;

hunted deer and rabbits; and gathered wild edible plants. They manufactured pottery as well as a wide variety of stone, bone, and wooden tools. The basic economic pattern upon which all subsequent Puebloan cultural development was based already existed.

Two additional villages on the Mesa Verde help to illustrate the pattern of late Basketmaker villages. Six pithouses in Step House Cave on Wetherill Mesa were built around A.D. 600 to 610. A second village at Twin Trees, less than 1,000 feet from Earth Lodge B, dates around 700 and might have housed succeeding generations from the older neighboring settlement. A larger than usual pithouse without typical domestic features may have been the scene of community-wide religious ceremonies for both villages.

While we still lack a complete picture of Basketmaker society on Mesa Verde, we do know these people lived in villages of from six to ten pithouses with attendant storage and work units. The members of each village shared not only daily interactions with one another, but also surrounding resources such as springs, farmland, wood supplies, and hunting and foraging territories. Wooden post stockades around two similar villages near Yellow Jacket indicate each village probably recognized its own identity.

Within the village, each pithouse probably sheltered an extended family—typically three generations descended from one married couple. Most likely, a husband and wife formed the core of this household with their children and widowed parents or siblings. Occasionally, a second married couple (either surviving parents, a married sibling, or a married child) might have been present. The total number of pithouse residents, which would have ranged from six to fifteen, was reflected by the size of the house. The members of each

household shared living quarters and cooperated in daily tasks revolving around food preparation and other survival needs. By watching and helping, children would have learned how to behave and to assist their parents with many activities.

Reconstructed pithouse, Step House Cave, 1967. Courtesy, Mesa Verde National Park (MVNP). Photo by Myron Wood.

EARLY PUEBLO SOCIAL REVOLUTION

The Basketmaker pattern of villages with 40 to 150 residents organized into extended family households seems to have been the culmination of a long period (perhaps up to 1,500 years) of societal stability. In contrast, the early Pueblo stages of Anasazi culture, from A.D. 750 to 1150, saw remarkable developments in architecture, in village planning, and in the social system. The architectural revolution of the Northern San Juan people began when outdoor storehouses and shaded work areas were connected into blocks of adjoining rooms. The people built walls by weaving branches through upright wooden posts and coating this foundation with mud. This form of construction is called "wattle and daub" or *jacal*. Upright sandstone slabs buttressed the lower walls of wattle and daub

structures. Their large living rooms abutted on to one another to form a row of buildings running east-west. Storerooms were attached on the north side of this row of living rooms and on the south side were roofed work spaces built in portico fashion. Pithouses at this time had become almost entirely subterranean, with their roofs forming part of the outdoor work area.

By the ninth century, we can recognize the emergence of what archaeologists term the *unit pueblo*—a block of living and storage rooms with a pithouse lying to the south. This unit design probably descended from the Basketmaker extended family household; however, the living rooms with hearths suggest the emergence of smaller subdivisions of nuclear families (parents and children) linked by kinship ties. Are we seeing here the origin of the lineages or clans found among the historic Pueblo Indians?

At this same time, clusters of unit pueblos, many adjoining one another, began to form much larger villages than are known from the earlier Basketmaker era. Archaeologists have excavated portions of such villages on Chapin Mesa at Twin Trees and on Wetherill Mesa at Badger House Community, and others are known from surveys. Our best pictures of whole villages, however, come from excavations in the surrounding area, such as Alkali Ridge and along the Dolores River Valley in the Montezuma Valley, and La Plata and Navajo reservoir districts to the east in the Northern San Juan. The largest of these villages were approximately double the size of the largest Basketmaker villages.

Following the establishment of the unit pueblo came other changes in construction. Between A.D. 900 and 1100, Northern San Juan builders began to use more sandstone masonry instead of wattle and

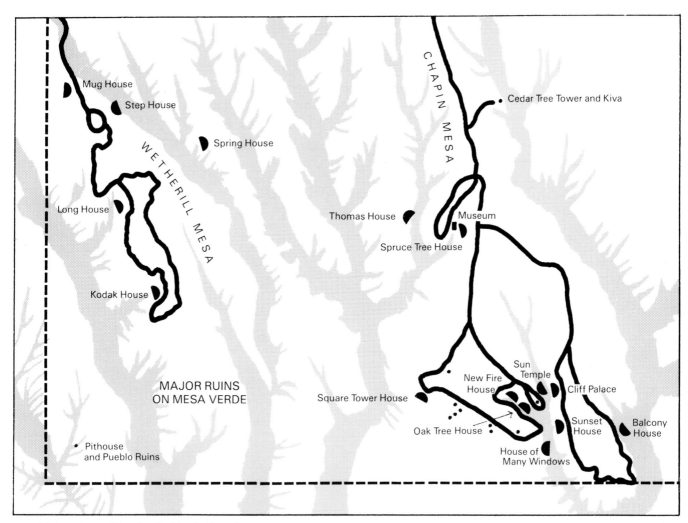

Major ruins on Mesa Verde. Map by Betsy James.

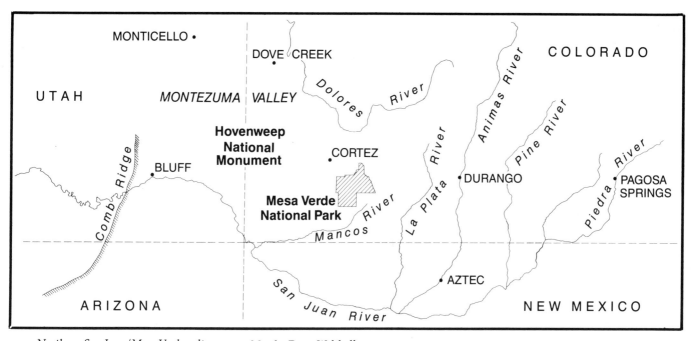

Northern San Juan/Mesa Verde culture area. Map by Dany Walthall.

daub, because it was stronger and more permanent. Many unit pueblos began to stand separately from one another, though still clustered into large villages. Interestingly, the pithouses became kivas, subterranean rooms in which ceremonies were held related to specific kinship groups.

A large variant of the small kin group constructions found in the largest villages is the so-called Great Kiva. These partly underground rooms exceeded forty feet in diameter and contained features similar to the smaller kivas. They have only recently been identified in the Northern San Juan region from as early as the 800s, a condition suggesting they probably evolved from the large ceremonial pithouses used by Basketmaker people. Great Kivas probably served as centers of ceremonial activities uniting a number of smaller communities with the larger villages. By the eleventh century, the largest of these villages had again doubled in population to around 400 persons. The

Far View ruins, 1984. Photo by Paul Logsdon.

best-known examples of such large villages occur at Far View on the Mesa Verde and the Ansel Hall (Cahone) site in the Montezuma Valley.

North court of Spruce Tree House. Courtesy, MVNP. Photo by Don Watson.

THE CLASSIC PUEBLO STAGE

By A.D. 1100, the population of the Northern San Juan region, had clearly concentrated in the Montezuma Valley. It appears that most people lived in large settlements such as Yellow Jacket, Lowry Ruins, and the Goodman Point Ruin, each of which had over 1,000 inhabitants. These large towns had either Great Kivas or distinctive "tri-wall" structures, both of which provided community meeting areas and places for rituals to be enacted. The valley population grew to around 30,000, while only about 2,500 lived on the Mesa Verde itself.

Though fewer in numbers, the Mesa Verde dwellers at this time had developed many ways to take advantage of their surroundings. On the Mesa Verde, the village at Far View that was first settled around A.D. 900 grew to a population of about 500 by the A.D. 1100s. The Far View people developed sophisticated ways to take advantage of the region's limited availability of water. They made their own water supply at Mummy Lake, an artificial reservoir capable of holding up to a half-million gallons of water. The reservoir was fed by a half-mile long system of collection ditches that also flowed into a canal bringing water to terraced farm plots. The Far View people cultivated farmland around their houses and on the mesa top immediately to the south. They also built stone terraces to create patches of fertile land in the ravines. Living in masonry apartment blocks, they held communal religious ceremonies in a kiva-and-tower combination structure built on the ruins of an older house.

About A.D. 1200, the residents of Far View moved ten miles south to become the core of a still larger community of people who built some thirty-three cliff dwellings in Cliff and Fewkes canyons. These include the well-known and magnificent ruins of Cliff Palace, Oak Tree House, Sunset House, New Fire House, and Mummy House. Altogether they contained close to 550 rooms and 60 kin group kivas, serving the 600 to 800 people who shared relatively close quarters in

South plaza of Balcony House, 1910. Courtesy, Museum of New Mexico. Photo by Jesse Nusbaum.

these two converging canyons. Fewer than ten trails led up the vertical sandstone cliffs from the cliff dwellings to the mesa-top farmland. Consequently, the occu-

pants of these villages would have seen their neighbors frequently as they walked to and from their fields, fetched water from the springs, or attended ceremonies at two communal ritual buildings, Sun Temple and Fire Temple. Fire Temple, a retangular form of the Great Kiva, was located by a spring that was purposefully enhanced by the flow of water trapped in an artificial reservoir above the spring. Water in the reservoir then percolated down through the sandstone bedrock and fed the spring's aquifer.

Mesa Verde's well-preserved cliff dwellings provide unusually accurate room and kiva estimates even without excavation. Consequently, we know the Cliff Canyon/Fewkes Canyon settlement housed about half of Chapin Mesa's population during the thirteenth century. The remaining people lived in four smaller villages and a number of hamlets scattered around Chapin Mesa. The four villages are represented

Cliff dwelling on the Ute Mountain Ute Reservation, 1984. Photo by Paul Logsdon.

7

Square Tower House. Courtesy, MVNP. Photo by Don Watson.

by Spruce Tree House, Square Tower House, Balcony House, and a group of sites at the head of Pool Canyon on the Ute Mountain Ute Indian Reservation to the south. Probably people from all over Chapin Mesa attended ceremonies at Sun Temple and Fire Temple.

On Wetherill Mesa, Long House probably represents the population center during the early thirteenth century. It stood four to five stories high in some places, had about 150 rooms, 21 kivas, and another rectangular Great Kiva. Work areas for tasks such as grinding corn, weaving, and tool- and basket-making were spread throughout the living area. Water seeped into the back of the cave and the

Long House people capitalized on this natural flow by pecking basins in the bedrock to collect the water. The nearby mesa top would have provided land on which corn and other crops were grown. Smaller villages, centered on such cliff dwelling sites as Spring House, Mug House, Kodak House, and Double House, seem to duplicate the pattern on Chapin Mesa of a larger center surrounded by smaller settlements.

In Johnson Canyon on the Ute Reservation, cliff dwellings such as Lion House and Hoy House were first built about A.D. 1130. These sites formed an outlying village to the Chapin Mesa people and were only occupied sporadically into the

1240s. Altogether, the Johnson Canyon cliff dwellings housed fewer people than Cliff Palace by itself.

In the Montezuma Valley, eight towns larger than the Cliff Canyon/Fewkes Canyon villages have been recognized. At the Lowry town, which traces its origins back to at least the ninth century, some 108 standardized residence units (each with a kin group kiva) cover almost one square mile. The housing units were arranged in two clusters around plazas on opposite sides of the water supply. Water came from a spring, an artificial reservoir, and a series of permanent natural pools in a shallow canyon between the house blocks. An estimated 1,800 persons lived at Lowry, using roads within the town and leading to outlying villages and farming areas. A Great Kiva, probably remodeled from an earlier structure, had been in use since A.D. 1106.

The largest town in Montezuma Valley was at Yellow Jacket. Occupation here can be traced back to the seventh century, but the town's size has obscured most details of its early development. Yellow Jacket contains roughly 1,800 rooms and probably had a population exceeding 2,500—equal to the estimated population for the entire Mesa Verde at its peak. The town contained streets, plazas with shrines, a managed water supply, and a very large Great Kiva.

The rural hinterland population surrounding Yellow Jacket consisted of eight villages of about 300 people each, plus numerous hamlets of 70 or fewer each. Several of the villages also had their own managed domestic water supply. A segment of roadway between two villages suggests that a network of roads may once have linked Yellow Jacket with its surrounding villages. Many pottery kilns, at least one isolated shrine, and terraced farmlands appear to have been part of this multicommunity unit. Yellow Jacket's Great Kiva and plazas may have drawn in excess of 5,000 people together for important ceremonial occasions. The remaining six towns, in order of size, were Sand Canyon Ruin, Goodman Point Ruin, Mud Springs, Yucca House, Lancaster Ruin, and Wilson Ruin. Each had either a Great Kiva or a tri-wall structure (a circular version of the Sun Temple).

The eight Montezuma Valley towns form a rough line running northwest to southeast, which would continue through the Mesa Verde's Cliff Canyon/Fewkes Canyon town, the contemporary sites of La Plata District (reported by Earl Morris), and terminate at Aztec Ruin on the Animas River in northwestern New Mexico. Aztec Ruin represents a large Pueblo II village into which a Chacoan group migrated during the late 1000s. By the late 1100s, the populations had amalgamated into a typical Northern San Juan town with both a Great Kiva and a tri-wall structure providing a communal ceremonial center.

Smaller population concentrations occurred elsewhere in the Montezuma Valley. At Hovenweep, six villages of 100 to 300 people each clustered around a slightly larger village at the Square Tower Group. All lay within one-half day's walk from the center. Other similar groups seem to have been distributed in Montezuma Canyon; along the San Juan River near Bluff, Utah; on Alkali Ridge; and near Blanding, Utah. Another group of villages in the valley between Cortez and Dolores, Colorado, were either independent or affiliates of the Mud Springs town.

The final overall pattern of social and political organization in the Northern San Juan is one of budding urban settlements functioning as ceremonial centers for surrounding, more rural populations. The towns range in population from roughly 1,000 to 2,500 and contain several features or buildings shared by all inhabitants—such as ceremonial buildings, streets, and water supply. In addition, the towns seem to have provided places to which outlying populations came for both ceremonial occasions and trading activities.

ABANDONMENT

The twelfth and thirteenth centuries in the Northern San Juan, including the Mesa Verde, saw the culmination of four centuries of relatively rapid development in social and political organization that verged on becoming an urban society. The small Basketmaker communities of extended family households had grown into much larger communities divided into kin groups of nuclear family households. Furthermore, a division of the community into two parts—a duality—had arisen. Thus, within four centuries, a two-level social system had evolved into one with at least four levels—nuclear household, kin group or lineage, dual parts, and community. A possible fifth level may

Lowry ruins (foreground) and Montezuma Valley, 1984. Photo by Paul Logsdon.

MESA VERDE MONTEZUMA VALLEY SETTLEMENT

A.D. 600 Basketmaker settlers established on the Mesa Verde; sedentary farming; pithouse dwellings in villages; earliest pottery; turkeys domesticated for feathers.

750 Beginning of Pueblo culture on the Mesa Verde; above-ground houses/unit pueblos; wattle and daub construction; deep pithouses; villages double in size; great kivas appear in Montezuma Valley.

900 Beginning of sandstone masonry, beginnings of the true kiva; Far View village established using Mummy Lake water storage system.

1100 Large towns concentrated in Montezuma Valley acting as ceremonial centers with great kivas and tri-walled structures; Far View population of 500; turkeys now used for food.

1200 Mesa Verdeans move to cliff dwellings. Cliff and Fewkes canyons settled; advancements in architecture and craft skills; general population growth in Northern San Juan region; Montezuma Valley towns reach up to 2,500 people each with total population estimated at 30,000.

by 1300 Abandonment of Mesa Verde and Northern San Juan region by Puebloan people.

have been emerging in the relationship between the ceremonial-trading center and its surrounding rural villages and hamlets. Then the growth ceased.

By around A.D. 1300, the entire San Juan drainage, including the Northern San Juan, had been abandoned by Puebloan peoples. They moved south and southeastward into the lands of the historic Hopi, Zuni, and Rio Grande pueblos. They retained the basic community organization; maximum size of towns never exceeded 2,500 to 3,000. Several towns had outlying smaller villages whose inhabitants returned to the towns for ceremonial occasions.

No one really understands why the Pueblos migrated out of the San Juan drainage during the thirteenth century. Drought, enemy incursions, pestilence, and internal feuding have all been suggested, but none have yet been verified. Whatever the reasons, the Pueblos did move away, and in the process they stabilized their social organization. To have developed beyond their thirteenth century achievements, they would have had to form social classes, develop craft specialties, and recognize an elite ruling class. Such developments would have led to a true urban society with towns and cities in excess of 3,000 people. Yet it did not happen. Perhaps the massive population relocation around A.D. 1300 enforced a kind of social stability. Or possibly the society refused to surrender its basic tenet of social equality. Certainly modern Pueblo society and government relies heavily on the value of egalitarianism, and no modern Pueblo exceeds a population of 3,000.

Arthur Rohn is an archaeologist and professor of anthropology at Wichita State University. He has conducted extensive research on the Mesa Verde and in the Northern San Juan region.

MESA VERDE: A Century of Research

By Alden C. Hayes

The Mesa Verde archaeological district occupies a magnificent slab of geography that has probably been subjected to more intensive investigation than any other area of comparable size north of Mexico. The green-mantled tableland that gave its name to the Mesa Verde branch of Anasazi culture lies near the center of the district, but it has been argued that the mesa itself was not the cultural hearth and, indeed, may have been the backwoods of the time. Be that as it may—and I don't concede it—the reasons for archaeologists' extra devotion to Mesa Verde are to be found in the re-markable preservation of material in the dry shelter caves and in the breath-taking setting. We have been trying for some time to establish ourselves as rational scientists to be taken every bit as seriously as physicists, geneticists and the other scholars who count and measure and discover natural laws. Still, the archaeologist who denies the romance and excitement of a first (or fiftieth) glimpse of a windowed wall of masonry, half hidden behind the piñon trees and hugging the face of a sandstone cliff, is probably not altogether honest.

Jesse Walter Fewkes at Far View excavations, 1916. Courtesy, MVNP. Photo by J. W. Fewkes.

I was smitten in 1958, when I was assigned to Mesa Verde National Park to make an archaeological survey as part of an extensive research project. My first cater-cornered view of Double House from the cliff above it gave me the thrill of discovery, though I knew hundreds had preceded me. During the next four years, I became acquainted, in person or through their works, with many who had come before me.

Those who got there first were not necessarily writers, nor written about, so Juan Maria Rivera may have been preceded, but according to our records, he was the first European to see Mesa Verde. In 1765, he came into the country from Santa Fe by way of the San Luis Valley and across the upper San Juan River to trade baubles to the Utes and Paiutes in exchange for unneeded children to be taken back to turn into Christian housemaids and sheepherders. He and other contemporary traders put names on the land, for when Frailes Francisco Atanasio Domínguez and Silvestre Vélez de Escalante came through from Santa Fe on the same route in 1776 to scout out a trail to San Francisco Bay, many features already had names and they named still more. The La Plata Mountains, the Abajos, the Dolores River, the Rio de los Mancos, and Mesa Verde itself all bore those names back in the 1700s. As far as we know, the friars did not climb the mesa, but Escalante, who was the diarist of the expedition, was interested in evidence of early inhabitants, and he described a ruined settlement on the south side of the Dolores River, which now carries his name.

Though it must have been familiar to the wide-ranging trappers of the 1830s, the earliest recorded Anglo-Americans to see this country were members of Captain J. N. McComb's party, who, in 1859, were one of several expeditions of that period dispatched by the U.S. Army to find an easy way to punch a railroad through to the Pacific coast. They did not find a feasible route in southwestern Colorado, but they camped between the foot of the Mesa Verde and the Mancos River— probably on Mud Creek—and Professor J. S. Newberry, the expedition's geologist, climbed Point Lookout on the Mesa's north scarp for a sweeping view of the Four Corners country, from Shiprock to the La Sal Mountains, the San Miguels, the La Platas, and back south to Huerfano Mesa.

In 1874, four large surveying parties, each with some federal backing were mapping and describing the terrain of the Far West. Lieutenant George M. Wheeler, under the sponsorship of the U.S. Corps of Topographical Engineers, was working east across Arizona and into northwestern New Mexico;

William H. Jackson (far right) with members of photographic division of the 1874 Hayden survey, readying for their first expedition into Colorado. Courtesy, Colorado Historical Society.

Major John Wesley Powell was completing his geological studies of the western Colorado Plateau; and Clarence King was writing the final reports of his "Fortieth Parallel Survey" from California across Nevada and Utah and to the Continental Divide in the Southern Rockies. The expedition of Dr. Ferdinand V. Hayden was the earliest, the largest, and most ambitious of the four. Expanded from a modest exploration of western Nebraska, the expedition over the years had claimed the Rocky Mountains as its domain for geographical studies. All four of the leaders were vying for the privilege of heading *the* single government agency responsible for western exploration.

After mapping and describing the wonders of Yellowstone National Park and the Tetons, Hayden was working south through Colorado and the ranges surrounding South Park when he became apprehensive that Wheeler was about to trespass on his territory. To forestall that unhappy possibility and to stake his claim, he sent his photographer, William H. Jackson, to the drainage of the San Juan River. While outfitting in Denver, Jackson heard from prospectors of mysterious empty houses built into caves in the sandstone cliffs, and he looked forward to seeing them. There was no settlement west of the La Plata Mountains at that time, but there was a small camp of about a dozen prospectors at "Parrott City" on the headwaters of the La Plata River, just over the ridge from the present-day town of Mancos. Jackson made his way from Durango to Parrott city, where he engaged the services of Captain John Moss, an experienced mountaineer who was the leading citizen of the camp, to show him the houses in the cliffs.

After a twenty-five to thirty mile ride, the six-man party made camp the first night deep in Mancos Canyon. They had ridden across several mounds of rubble covered with sherds of pottery but had seen nothing of any real interest, so it was in a spirit both rueful and playful that, while digesting the evening's beans and sowbelly, they teased one of the packers about having to tote the heavy boxes of photographic equipment up the canyon wall to the apparently nonexistent cliff house. "He asked us to point out the spot," Jackson's diary reads. "The Captain pointed at random. 'Yes,' said he [the packer], 'I see it.' And behold upon my close observation there was something that appeared very like a house." Despite the failing light, they scrambled up the steep and brushy talus slope and over successive benches of perpendicular sandstone to investigate the little cliff dwelling that Jackson named, and we know today, as Two Story Cliff House. In better light the next morning, they returned with the unwieldly camera and 11 by 14 glass plates and made the first pictures of a Mesa Verde cliff dwelling. Accompanying Jackson was a young correspondent for the *New York Tribune*, Ernest Ingersoll (for Hayden knew the power of publicity), and Ingersoll's story along with Jackson's illustrated report quickly kindled an interest among the scholarly, as well as the merely curious, that has not diminished.

The following year, 1875, Professor Hayden sent one of his principal topographers, William Henry Holmes, to make a more detailed study of the area. Holmes was a geologist, an artist, and a skilled cartographer. He climbed Mesa Verde to make a beautiful projected drawing of the country that included the southern tip of the mesa, Ute Mountain, and the Abajos. He discovered several other cliff houses and made the first known excavation when he scratched a prehistoric pot out of the dust at Sixteen-Window House. Holmes's experiences so stimulated his interests in Indian antiquities that a few years later he left the Geological Survey to spend the rest of his working years as an archaeologist with the Bureau of American Ethnology and the U.S. National Museum.

Other results of the Hayden Survey were papers by E. A. Barber on Indian pottery and stone artifacts, and by Alfred Morgan on various archaeological aspects of the survey. There were other Morgans in the vicinity in the late 1870s, for L. H. Morgan, the distinguished ethnologist and honorary Iroquois, made a lightning visit in 1878 and wrote a paper on Aztec Ruin on the Animas River. He was certainly the first trained anthropologist to visit the area. He was accompanied by his grandnephew, W. F. Morgan, who wrote a detailed description of a small cliff house.

All of the activity in the decade following Jackson's description of Two Story House was a matter of men following each other's footprints and seeing the same little ruins over and over. The inner recesses of the Mesa Verde were still unknown—or at least unadvertised. S. E. Osborne, a miner, left his name in Hemenway House in 1885, and Mrs. Virginia McClurg of Denver, who was later to become the main mover behind the establishment of Mesa Verde National Park, was in Balcony House in 1886. It is hard to believe that a prospector looking for gold had not stumbled on Cliff Palace, or that a cowboy looking for a waterhole had not found the spring in Long House, but few prospectors and cattlemen are geared to talk or write about things other than mines or cattle. The Wetherills expanded the scope—and talked about it.

In 1880, Benjamin K. Wetherill, a former Indian agent and a rancher, moved to the Mancos Valley via Oklahoma and Kansas with his wife, daughter, and five sons to settle a ranch at the edge of the Ute reservation a few miles downstream from the newly established town of Mancos. Wetherill, a Quaker, had always gotten along well with Indians, and he soon made friends of the Utes, who allowed him to graze his cattle on their country.

Wetherill's sons had been running the family cattle for eight years in Mancos Canyon and its tributaries when, on a cold day in December 1888, the oldest son, Richard and his brother-in-law,

The Wetherills at a Ute wedding party in 1891 or 1892 in Mancos, Colorado. Richard is at far left; Benjamin, fourth from left; Al, center. Courtesy, New Mexico State Records Center and Archives.

Charlie Mason, were following cow tracks up the southern end of the *potrero* we now call Chapin Mesa. They came out onto a stretch of slick rock on the rim of a canyon, and gazing across the gulch through flurries of snow, they were amazed to see a great cave totally filled with houses—tier upon tier of them. The boys had been digging in the small ruins for relics in their spare time for years and may have become a bit blasé, but this thing overwhelmed them. The cow tracks were forgotten while they explored the ruin they dubbed "The Cliff Palace," and the next day they discovered Spruce Tree House and Square Tower House. The third day they had to return to the line camp at the mouth of Johnson Canyon, but Richard came back to spend most of the winter digging in Cliff Palace and Spruce Tree House. For him, the cattle business was never again the same.

Richard made a large collection that winter of 1888–89. It did not require a great deal of earth moving, because many of the rooms had been abandoned, with household gear still sitting where it had been left—cooking pots on the hearths, food bowls on the floors, sandals in the corners, and digging sticks thrust under vigas by doorways. Feeling that the world needed to know about his discoveries, he boxed up his collection and took it by wagon to Durango, where it was exhibited in a hotel lobby. To his disappointment, his treasures elicited little interest. All of the local people occasionally picked up arrowheads—this was just more old Indian stuff. So Richard took his relics to Pueblo, hoping to rouse a little more interest, but Puebloans, too, were chiefly centered on mines and livestock. One more showing, this time in Denver, was more successful, and the entire collection was sold to the Colorado Historical Society.

Back at the ranch, the Wetherills had a visitor in the summer of 1889. Frederick H. Chapin, a New England man of means and a member of the Hartford Archaeological Society, had traveled extensively in the West and was acquainted with members of Hayden's survey. From them, and from Jackson's and Holmes's publications, he knew of the cliff dwellings on the Mancos River and had determined to see them. After a trip to the mines at Ouray, he came down through Silverton into Durango, where he had difficulty even getting directions to Mancos, let alone any information about the ruins. Finally reaching the Mancos Valley by rented trap, by blind luck he found lodging at Wetherill's Alamo Ranch. He was taken by Richard and John Wetherill on an extended inspection trip down the Mancos, up onto Red Mesa south of the river, and then up onto Mesa

Verde. He was so intrigued by the ruins that he returned the following summer and in 1892 his popular book, *The Land of the Cliff Dwellers*, was published—the first detailed popular account.

The second collection of "relics" made by the Wetherill brothers, in the winter of 1889–90, was sold to an Illinois firm that exhibited it at the Field Columbian Exposition in Chicago in 1893. It was then purchased by Phoebe Hearst who donated the artifacts to the University of Pennsylvania Museum—except for a few pieces that she took home to California, where they eventually ended up at the university's museum in Berkeley.

Another wealthy tenderfoot landed at Alamo Ranch in June 1891. Gustav Nordenskiold, the 23-year-old son of a titled Swedish scientist and Arctic explorer, was touring frontier America to seek a cure for his tuberculosis, happened into Denver, and saw the Wetherill's exhibit at the museum. His interest whetted, he arrived at B. K. Wetherill's homestead just a few days later, planning to make a quick inspection of the ruins. The few days he had intended to stay stretched into months. With Alfred or John Wetherill as guides, or less frequently, with Richard or Clayton, he explored the cliff dwellings, especially the lesser-known west side of the mesa. Nordenskiold introduced systematic investigation to the mesa, bringing to an end the period of "gee whiz" discovery. He taught his guides, and Richard in particular, to move slowly with whisk broom and

Gustav Nordenskiold. Courtesy, MVNP.

trowel, to record proveniences, and to label the artifacts removed. He made excavations in several ruins—rather extensive ones in Step House—and made the first orderly listing and numbering of sites. The maps, drawings, and photographs in his lavishly illustrated *The Cliff Dwellers of Mesa Verde*, published in Sweden in 1893 in both Swedish and English, still are valuable sources of information. Nordenskiold was also the first to perceive culture change and stratigraphically revealed chronology, when he noted in lower levels of refuse at Step House a type of crude pottery that was perhaps ". . .the work of a people who inhabited the Step House cave before the erection of the cliff village." Three years later, the young scholar died of the disease that brought him to Colorado. The valuable collection he made that summer remains intact in the National Museum of Helsinki, Finland.

The Wetherill's direct impact on Mesa Verde diminished after 1893, as they began to look for fresher fields to the west. In Cottonwood Canyon in southeastern Utah, Richard found evidence of a pre-ceramic occupation below the masonry houses of the cliff dwellers, confirming Nordenskiold's hunch. He first called them the "Basket People," and later referred to them as the "Basket Makers." It was Richard also who introduced other terms we use today: "Cliff Dweller" and "Anasazi."

In 1895, his last year on Alamo Ranch before moving to Chaco Canyon, Richard Wetherill was once more host and guide to an eastern visitor. Dr. T. Mitchell Prudden, a physician and professor of pathology at Columbia University, for several years had spent his summers exploring the West. The writings of Jackson, Chapin, and Nordenskiold drew him naturally to seek out the Wetherills on the Mancos River. Prudden's 1895 visit marked the beginning of nearly two decades of excursions, resulting in many articles, both popular and scientific, on the antiquities of the Southwest. Following the excavation of a series of mounds on McElmo Creek near Cortez at the northwest foot of Mesa Verde, he made his most substantial contribution—the concept of the "unit-pueblo" (the small cluster of rooms associated with a single kiva) and the delineation of a stage preceding the building of the more complex Classic structures.

The more adventuresome tourists continued to be packed up onto the mesa, but for the next ten or eleven years nothing of any archaeological importance happened. Then in 1906, Mesa Verde National Park was established. Influential in its establishment was Edgar Lee Hewett, who helped

Edgar Lee Hewett at Mesa Verde. Photo by Fred Campora. Courtesy, Museum of New Mexico, neg. no. 44296.

draft the legislation as well as the Antiquities Act, also passed in that same year.

Hewett has not been acclaimed by his peers or those who followed as an outstanding practitioner of the archaeologist's trade, but none will deny his considerable beneficial influence in two areas—the preservation of archaeological resources in parks and monuments, and the training of archaeologists. A list of those who studied or apprenticed under him almost outlines a history of southwestern archaeology. In a little book of reminiscences, Hewett explained his theory of education. Once in Chicago down near the lakeshore he watched a gang of wharf rats, under the guidance of an older boy, jumping off the dock to swim. He asked their leader, "How did these boys learn to swim so well?" "I taught 'em," he was told. "How did you teach them?" Hewett asked. "Push 'em off the pier," was the reply. Hewett felt that this was also the best technique for teaching archaeology, and he was still pushing students off the pier in his last year at the University of New Mexico in 1935.

Jesse L. Nusbaum (left) and Alfred V. Kidder above Spruce Tree House, 1908. Courtesy, Faith Kidder Fuller.

The secretary of the interior, impressed by Hewett's work on the legislation involving Mesa Verde and the Antiquities Act, asked him to make a survey of the Four Corners country to see what other sites might need protection. Hewett's School of American Research, then still the western wing of the Archaeological Institute of America, had been operating a field school (the first of its kind) on the Pajarito Plateau west of Santa Fe. To work on the Four Corners survey in 1907, he brought to the Mesa Verde area two candidates for "pushing" who were to make names for themselves. He met Sylvanus G. Morley, a Harvard undergraduate from Buena Vista, Colorado, and Alfred V. Kidder, another Harvard boy from New England, at Holly's Ranch in McElmo Canyon after their long ride from Mancos. The next morning, the three climbed the mesa above the juncture of Yellowjacket and McElmo canyons, a vantage point from which one can see some of the biggest country in the west: from Shiprock in New Mexico, to the Carrizo Mountains in Arizona, the Henrys and La Sals in Utah, and to Mesa Verde and the La Platas in Colorado. With a vague wave of his arm, he instructed them to make an archaeological survey and promised to return in six weeks.

In spite of this rugged initiation, Kidder and Morley were game enough to have another shot at it the following year. Hewett set Vay Morley to excavating Cannonball Ruin on the edge of McElmo Canyon and put Kidder up on Mesa Verde with a new recruit, 20-year-old Jesse Logan Nus-

baum, a gangling string bean from Greeley, Colorado. With Nusbaum taking pictures and Kidder making sketch maps, they were to record all the major cliff dwellings. The boys were agile. In 1960, I located a pretty little cliff dwelling near the tip of Long Mesa so difficult of access that I had reason to hope it had not been entered since the Indians left it. After rigging a lightweight, portable rope ladder, with some trouble we entered the south end of the cave to be confronted by an inscription on the sandstone wall reading "J. Nusbaum, 1908."

Morley's report of his Cannonball excavation appeared first in the *American Anthropologist*, with what today seems incredible speed—in the fall of the same year the digging was done. It was reprinted as Number 2 in the *Papers of the School of American Archaeology* in Santa Fe, one of the first accounts of a southwestern excavation by an American archaeologist published in the United States. In his report Morley went beyond a mere description of the architecture to speculate on social units and on the building of the large complex by accretion of groups of domestic rooms around a kiva.

The School of American Research had one more year in Mesa Verde country in 1910, when Hewett brought Nusbaum back to clean up and stabilize Balcony House. Not only a professional photographer, Nusbaum had also been apprenticed to his father, a bricklayer, and the results of his summer's work still stand. When the work was completed in the fall, Nusbaum dismissed his crew

Sylvanus G. Morley, ca. 1910. Courtesy, Museum of New Mexico (neg. no. 10313).

but, though low on supplies, he stayed on with one man to await Dr. Hewett's inspection of the work. Hewett finally rode in one afternoon so late they had to build fires to illuminate the ruin. He had come from Mancos without extra horses for his men and insisted on riding off the mesa in the dark that same evening. He left in a swirling snowstorm, leaving Nusbaum and his helper to make their way on foot the next morning. Without breakfast, they floundered through snowdrifts over the north rim and into Cortez, arriving well after midnight.

Dr. Jesse Walter Fewkes, of the Bureau of American Ethnology, is quoted in Sylvanus Morley's report of the Cannonball dig in regards to the sipapu in the kivas. The two undoubtedly met that summer of 1908, the first of many that Fewkes was to spend on Mesa Verde. After more than twenty years experience in the Southwest as an ethnologist and archaeologist, principally in Arizona, he came to the Mesa Verde area to excavate and stabilize Spruce Tree House. Although picked over by many previous visitors, the site yielded a sizable collection, the first artifacts from Mesa Verde to be housed in the National Museum. In 1909, he returned to uncover and reinforce the crumbling walls of Cliff Palace.

After years of ethnographic research among the Hopis, excavations in the Salt River Valley and at Zuni for the Hemenway Expedition, explorations on the Mogollon Rim and in the Little Colorado Valley, and stabilization work at Casa Grande for the bureau, Mesa Verde was almost a retirement job for Fewkes. By this time, he was a rather benign looking fellow with a white beard below mahogany cheekbones, and white curls spilling out from under his Stetson. Most of his work was done by crews of Navajos and local ranchers while Fewkes explained things to the visitors. In 1915, while excavating Sun Temple, he inaugurated evening campfire programs at which he drew parallels between the architectural features and Hopi ethnographic data. He started the excavation of the Far View Ruin in 1916, and excavated Pipe Shrine House in 1922—his last year in the park.

Fewkes was a great detractor of the Wetherills, accusing them of desecrating and vandalizing the ruins. Of course, in 1888 hardly anybody knew how to get the information out of a ruin. Richard Wetherill's notes were as useful as Fewkes's annual reports to the Smithsonian, which were mainly devoted to the number of men employed and the number of rooms cleaned out, with a few comments on finds of particular interest—preliminary reports not followed by final ones. Unfortunately, almost no useful information was recorded in fifteen seasons of fieldwork. Fewkes did make a major contribution, however. He initiated and pioneered the business of ruins stabilization.

In his next to final year at Mesa Verde, Fewkes made another contribution. He complained to Stephen Mather, the director of the National Park Service, about the shoddy way the park was being run, accusing the ranger and his father-in-law, the park's superintendent, of looting the ruins and selling the plunder. After a tour of inspection accompanied by Dr. Fewkes, Mather relieved the superintendent and appointed Jesse Nusbaum, who had just completed the excavation of DuPont Cave near Kanab, Utah, for the Museum of the American Indian.

Nusbaum was not only an able administrator and a trained archaeologist, he had also learned something from his old mentor, Edgar Hewett, about enlisting help from those who were in a position to be helpful. In 1924, he devoted two days to guiding John D. Rockefeller, Jr. and his sons around the mesa. Rockefeller took a lively interest in plans for the development of the park and the establishment of a museum, pledging funds to help get something started. All of Fewkes's collections had gone to the National Museum, and there was almost nothing of the Anasazi arts to display. Partly to rectify that lack, Nusbaum elected to re-excavate Step House. This site also promised to provide information about the earlier inhabitants of the mesa, whose presence Nordenskiold had suspected—the people whom Richard Wetherill had labeled "Basket Makers," and whom Nusbaum himself had investigated in DuPont Cave in Utah. In the fall of 1924, he trained his crew by excavating undisturbed trash in the back of Spruce Tree House, and in February 1926, he packed out to Wetherill Mesa to camp on the rim and to work in Step House, where he cleaned out Basketmaker pithouses and definitely established the early use of cave sites. From Step House and from excavation in already worked-over ruins in Fewkes Canyon, at Bone Awl and Hoot Owl House on Moccasin Mesa, and Kodak House and Ruins 11, 11½, 12 and 16 on Wetherill, he gathered enough material to start the museum.

Government was easier in those days. If supervision was loose enough for it to be possible to hire relatives and make a commercial venture out of a government post, the same casual supervision also made it easier to do things for the public good. Nusbaum's budget was not broken down for him into minute categories— so many dollars to pick up beer bottles and so many to build trails. He had a lump sum to operate the park, plus whatever he could scrounge. Without having to submit plans to a remote office of civil servant engineers and architects, he was able to build of stone and timber, a headquarters, a museum, and residences for staff, using local workmen, and without reference to volumes of regulations.

About the same time that Nusbaum was being reintroduced to Mesa Verde, another archaeologist began a long series of excavations in the area. Paul Martin started digging near the head of Yellowjacket Canyon north of Cortez in the summer of 1928. He was at first sponsored by the Colorado State Historical Society and later by Chicago's Field Museum of Natural History. Martin's many competent, descriptive, and promptly published reports became a body of information that, along with Earl Morris's Animas River and Red Mesa work, made it possible to define a Mesa Verde Culture Area as distinct from other focal hearths in the Southwest.

Earl Morris had been a student at Hewett's field school on Pajarito Plateau, along with Kidder, Nusbaum, and Morley. In 1913, on Hewett's recommendation, the University of Colorado entrusted Morris with a few dollars for investigations of ruins on the mesa country between the La Plata and Mancos rivers. He returned to the same general vicinity and the nearby Animas Valley

every summer for the next twenty-one years, interrupted only by brief excursions into Canyon del Muerto, the Lukachukai Mountains, or to Yucatan. No better trowel hand, reader of dirt, or keener observer has to date searched the earth between the San Juan and the Dolores. He wrote well, could draw, and he remembered what he had seen and knew what it probably meant. Since he published his La Plata Valley report, a couple of generations of archaeologists have thought they had run on to something new, only to find that Morris had made the same observation fifty years before. Most of his work was under the auspices of the American Museum of Natural History, and for that institution he excavated and stabilized Aztec Ruin on the Animas in New Mexico and reconstructed the great kiva at that large pueblo.

On the basis of Morris's success at stabilizing the walls of Aztec and of Mummy Cave in Arizona, he was hired by the Park Service in 1935 to patch up the work done in Cliff Palace and Spruce Tree House by Fewkes some years before. To help him mix mud and lay rock, he hired James A. Lancaster, who had prior experience working for archaeologists in the area.

When Paul Martin first came down from Denver to dig near Ackmen (now Pleasant View), he took on a crew of local bean farmers to help him. One of those was Al Lancaster, who showed a remarkable aptitude and great enthusiasm for the work.

James A. Lancaster, 1963. Courtesy, MVNP. Photo by Fred Mang.

Lancaster became dig foreman and was on tap for succeeding summers. The summer of 1931, Paul was unable to return to the field. J. O. Brew, planning to come out from Harvard to excavate on Alkali Ridge near Blanding, Utah, wrote Martin asking for the names of men he might use. Paul had no hesitation in recommending Lancaster. Al made a valuable hand for Brew and stayed with him through the three seasons of work in a series of open sites on Alkali Ridge. When Paul was gearing up for a return to his work around Yellowjacket, he learned that his skilled foreman had transferred his allegiance to J. O. Brew and Harvard—that lodged a thorn of resentment in Martin that he never forgot.

After learning the rudiments of ruins stabilization from Earl Morris at Cliff Palace in 1935, Al put in the next four field seasons at the ruins of the Hopi Village of Awatovi for J. O. Brew again, who called him "the best field man the Southwest has produced." He returned to Mesa Verde in 1939 to take charge of a continuing program of stabilization and maintenance of the park's excavated sites. Lancaster had a part to play in almost all research on Mesa Verde from that time on—even after his so-called retirement in 1964.

What was known about cultural sequence and change at Mesa Verde by 1940 was largely by inference, drawing on the work of Martin, Morris, and Brew in adjacent valleys and on their separating ridges. Except for Nusbaum's Modified Basketmaker pithouses in Step House cave, and a pithouse excavated on Chapin Mesa by Ralph Linton in 1919, while he was assisting Fewkes, excavation on the mesa was mostly confined to the cliff dwellings and large surface ruins of the Classic or Great Pueblo period. In 1939 and 1940, Lancaster and Terah Smiley, of the University of Arizona, added to Basketmaker material by digging more pithouses on Chapin Mesa.

Nusbaum, who had been appointed consulting archaeologist to the secretary of the interior with his office in Santa Fe, was touring the park in 1939, when he spied bulldozers at work in Soda Canyon far below the mesa's rim on Ute Reservation land. Knowing the floor of the canyon to be paved with ruins, he protested to the superintendent of the Ute agency, and by threatening to phone Secretary Harold Ickes about the matter, he was able to get the road work halted until some salvage archaeology could be performed. This was a landmark episode. It set the precedent for the archaeological salvage work being done today, establishing government responsibility for conserving antiquities on government land. The road work was held up for two years until funds could

be found to support investigation of the archaeological sites in the right-of-way—the nation's first highway salvage project was born.

Erik K. Reed was sent up from the Santa Fe office of the National Park Service in the spring of 1942 to do the job. Reed's excavations in five sites and his survey of Mancos Canyon, just below Mesa Verde's southern toe, provided the basis for an attempt to describe a sequential development that could apply also to the archaeology on the mesa itself.

Harold Gladwin was a weathly, retired industrialist who, having found it difficult to get positive answers to his questions about the prehistoric Southwest, set up a foundation he called Gila Pueblo. He hired archaeologists and proceeded to look for answers, starting his search in central Arizona and working outward in ever-widening circles. Although his team collected tree-rings from many sites on and around the mesa in the mid-1930s, it was not until 1947 that he was prepared to put a shovel into the ground. To do the digging, he dispatched Deric O'Bryan, a man who knew the park well. O'Bryan, Jesse Nusbaum's step-son, had lived on the mesa as a boy, accompanying Jesse on the Step House dig and other expeditions.

Martin had dug around Yellowjacket hoping to establish a cultural sequence, and on Alkali Ridge Brew had looked for evidence of stages between the Modified Basketmaker and the Classic Pueblo, but previous work on Mesa Verde itself had been mostly reportorial and descriptive: "This is what we found." On his return to Mesa Verde, O'Bryan came with a list of nine questions he hoped to answer. Problem-oriented archaeology had arrived at Mesa Verde. Among the things he wanted to know were: What was the evidence on the mesa of the Paleoindian hunters, of the postulated Basketmaker I, or of the pre-ceramic agriculturists of Basketmaker II? How did the Modified Basketmakers of Mesa Verde compare to those of adjacent areas? Is there a locally definable Pueblo II or early Developmental Pueblo? And what caused the abandonment of the entire region at about A.D. 1300? Over the next two summers, O'Bryan made extensive excavations at four sites, showing a continuous occupation from the Modified Basketmaker of the seventh century up into the Great Pueblo period of the twelfth, providing answers to some of his questions and allowing him to propose a sequence of five phases of the progression—a system that has stood up fairly well in the light of evidence uncovered by subsequent work.

O'Bryan's excavations made apparent the gradual changes in architecture and in minor arti-

Douglas Osborne with artifacts from Wetherill Mesa, 1962. Courtesy, MVNP. Photo by Fred Mang.

facts, but the park did not have examples of the earlier stages to show to its visitors. Don Watson, the Park Archaeologist in 1950, with Al Lancaster by his side, completed an intensive survey of the sites on Chapin Mesa and located several good prospects for filling the gap. He and Lancaster, with the help of others on staff—Philip Van Cleave and Jean Pinkley—excavated four sites on the Ruins Loop Road between headquarters and the view point across the canyon from Cliff Palace. The purpose of the excavations was primarily to provide "exhibits-in-place" as adjuncts to the park's interpretive program, but they did more than that. They were also good digs that provided valuable information.

For four years, starting in 1953, Robert and Florence Lister ran a field school in archaeology at Mesa Verde for the University of Colorado, during which a series of Pueblo III houses in the vicinity of Far View were excavated. The digs and their stabilized walls fulfilled three objectives: they provided on-the-job training in field techniques for their students, they enriched the body of data, and they made additional exhibits to show to the park visitors. Bob Lister, like several of his predecessors, had a link to Mesa Verde in that he had been a student of Edgar L. Hewett at the University of New Mexico.

In 1958, the National Park Service undertook what

was perhaps the first large-scale multi-disciplinary research project in the United States when it fielded the Wetherill Mesa Archaeological Project, conceived by Chief Park Archaeologist John Corbett, and supervised by Douglas Osborne. The ostensible reason for the project, and the excuse for the expenditure of government funds, was the preparation of ruins for public exhibit on the west side of the park to help accommodate the crowded conditions caused by increased traffic. Of course, archaeologists were hoping to learn more about what happened a thousand years ago, and why. Generous support from the National Geographic Society helped with the theoretical, or less immediately pragmatic aspects of the project.

Between 1958 and 1965, the Park Service accomplished an intensive survey of Wetherill Mesa, and excavated and stabilized Mug House as well as Long House, the second largest cliff dwelling in the park. Step House was re-excavated, with the discovery of more pithouses, and prepared for exhibit. Five mesa-top sites exemplifying occupations from the mid-600s to the mid-1200s were excavated, and testing was done in a half-dozen more. Needed stabilization was also done in several other large cliff dwellings on Wetherill Mesa. The year-round crew of about fifteen (including laboratory help) was expanded to about fifty in the summer. Included in the permanent staff

Arthur H. Rohn in Mug House, 1960. Courtesy, MVNP. Photo by David Hannah.

Alden C. Hayes on ledge overlooking Park Canyon, 1963. Courtesy, MVNP. Photo by Fred Mang.

were George S. Cattanach, Arthur H. Rohn, and Richard P. Wheeler. Al Lancaster was still digging as well as supervising all the stabilization work. And Edgar Hewett's long arm was still reaching to Mesa Verde through Doug Osborne and me. Like Lister, we were Hewett's students during his last year on the campus at the University of New Mexico.

Following the completion of the Wetherill Mesa Project in 1965, we knew in much finer detail *what* happened at Mesa Verde, but certainly many questions remained about *why*. To probe some of those questions, Lister returned with his research team from the University of Colorado. Much of their work involved survey and salvage excavation for the Bureau of Land Management and the Ute Mountain Reservation. Also several sites were dug at the east side of the park where the Park Service planned expanded camping facilities. The team continued to look for answers to questions that archaeologists had been asking for years, such as, "What factors had contributed to the wholesale abandonment of the Four Corners area?" And, because every new addition to our knowledge through excavation gives rise to new questions, another arose: "In what ways was Mesa Verde culture affected by the rise of the 'Chaco Phenomenon?' "

A signal accomplishment of the University of Colorado was the completion of a rod-by-rod survey of the park. A project started by Don Watson in the 1930s and continued on the west side of the mesa by the Wetherill Mesa Project, still left three-quarters of the park unsurveyed. Nearly a century after Jackson's discovery of Two Story Cliff House, we still did not know how many archaeological sites we had, to say nothing of their location or type. Back in 1959, Park Superintendent Chester A. Thomas put on a show-and-tell program for local officials, newsmen, and chambers of commerce to describe the Wetherill Mesa research. After saying a few words about the survey I was conducting, I was asked by a nice young lady with note pad and pencil at the ready, "Mr. Hayes, how many undiscovered ruins are there in Mesa Verde?" Now, thanks to the exhaustive work of Park Research Archaeologist Jack E. Smith, one could answer that question, "Ma'am, there are none."

Alden Hayes is a senior archaeologist, formerly with the National Park Service, who has conducted research throughout the Southwest including on the Mesa Verde.

HOVENWEEP
Through Time

By Joseph C. Winter

I met the old man at the bridge across the Yellowjacket. Earlier in the week I had been introduced to him at Ismay's Trading Post in the southeastern corner of Utah, and when he learned that I was an archaeologist working at Hovenweep National Monument, he offered to take me to see the "other" Hovenweep.

"Those ruins at the monument are mighty fine," he said, "and Holly has some of the prettiest towers in the world, but there's a lot more to Hovenweep—come on, I'll show you." Though I had

Holly ruins. Photo by David Noble

explored the outback areas in the vicinity before, I'd done it without an oldtimer for a guide. I took him up on the offer.

We walked to his truck and drove north on a dirt road that led beyond the monument boundaries to a boulder at the foot of a cliff. The rock was covered with petroglyphs—strange humpbacked figures, geometric designs, and creatures the old man called "Corn Heads"—tall, big-footed men with long penises hanging down between their legs and corn plants in place of heads. There were Corn Head women too, with babies in their stomachs, and other big-footed people, raising their huge hands in the air.

"With their feet on the earth and their hands in the sky," said the old man, "or, at least, that's what a Ute Indian once told me." Then he broached a theory he was sure of, one I could neither prove or disprove. "You know what? All this is a great big newspaper or bulletin board where Indians left messages for one another and offered prayers to their gods. And they came from up there," he pointed to the ridge above us, "from up on top of Cannonball Mesa."

Then my guide told me about the ruins on the mesa and how we could drive to them in his truck. We turned around and followed the road to a jeep trail. When we reached the top, I discovered that the west end of the mesa narrowed to a neck with an ancient, high masonry wall built across it. Behind the wall were scores of slab-lined pithouse depressions dug down through the thin topsoil into the bedrock. Tens of thousands of potsherds covered the ground. Next, we drove to the north end of the mesa where the crumbling thirteenth-century towers of Cannonball Ruins looked much the same as they had seventy-six years ago when Sylvanus Morley excavated them and realized that they had been used by a Mesa Verde-like culture.

The next day I again met the old man at the bridge and was escorted on a long looping tour that covered the Hovenweep area from south to north. First, we drove down McElmo Creek to check out a large cluster of towers near its juncture with the San Juan River. Then, we continued to Montezuma Canyon, where we climbed to the rim and explored a fortified pithouse village. After that, we drove northeast up Cross Canyon to find the towers of McLean Basin, and finally we proceeded to the northern bean fields to inspect a series of Hovenweep sites: Big Spring House; Painted Hand; Risley Spring; the giant rubble mounds; the Prudden Units (small pueblos); the burned towers at Charnel House; the Herren Farm sites; Little Dog Ruins; and Beartooth Pueblo.

Petroglyphs near Cannonball Mesa. Photo by Joseph Winter.

My guide had to work in his fields for a few days, but when he reappeared, he took me to the great kivas and excavated pithouses on the ends of the ridges of the Ackmen-Lowry area and to the spectacular towers and pueblos that comprise Cajon Ruin. When he was finished, I took him to Hovenweep National Monument and the ruins of Cutthroat Castle, Holly House, Horseshoe House, Hackberry House, Square Tower, Twin Towers, Hovenweep Castle, Stronghold House, and Cajon Springs. I told him about the reservoirs and check dams and described my own archaeological excavations and surveys. I showed him the solstice portholes in the stone towers and explained our findings about the Holly ruin calendar. By the end of my tour, I think I had told the old man just about everything I knew about how the people of Hovenweep had lived.

That was in 1976, my last working summer at Hovenweep. Since then, I've returned every year, but just to look, not to dig. I've also kept abreast of archaeologists' discoveries in other valleys of the western Mesa Verde region, such as Sand Canyon, the Upper Yellowjacket, and the Dolores. Here is how I think Hovenweep fits into the geographic and cultural puzzle:

Hovenweep, a Ute word meaning "Deserted Valley," is actually a series of small river valleys that feed into lower McElmo Creek and the San Juan River. These tributaries include the western halves of the Yellowjacket, Hovenweep, Bridge, Ruin, and Cross drainages as well as the lower part of the Montezuma drainage. The long, box-shaped Cajon Mesa formed by this drainage system slopes gently from an elevation of 7,000 feet in the northern piñon-juniper forests and bean fields of the Ackmen-Lowry area to 4,400 feet in the shadscale-bush–covered benches and river flats along McElmo Creek and the San Juan. Cajon Mesa forms a cultural as well as natural unit: it is situated between the Yellowjacket area on the east, the Dolores on the north, and the Montezuma on the west. The entire area forms part of the Mesa Verde/Anasazi cultural region.

HOVENWEEP'S EARLIEST INHABITANTS

Human use of the 500-square-mile Cajon Mesa began some 14,000 years ago in the era of the big game hunters, when Paleoindians camped around several water sources, including Cajon Springs at the south end of the mesa. This large spring with its excellent overlook was apparently a favored hunting locale for thousands of years. However, although we know that some Paleoindians visited the mesa, our knowledge about their culture and way of life at Hovenweep is very limited.

The Paleoindian nomads were followed in about 5000 B.C. by small, seminomadic bands of hunters and gatherers who, like their predecessors, left clues about their existence primarily in the form of occasional scatters of stone tools and weapons. Archaeologists refer to these people as the Archaic or Desert Culture, and they have found ample evidence of their camps at Hovenweep on ridges above springs and at canyon heads. Their foraging sites have also been found in the upper Dolores Valley, just north of Hovenweep, and in other adjacent areas to the south, east, and west. The Hovenweep Archaic population (mainly of the Oshara Tradition) was probably part of a thinly spread but extensive population who foraged all across the northern San Juan Basin and adjacent drainages.

In light of the fact that after approximately A.D. 1 the entire Four Corners region became dominated by Anasazi farmers living in settled villages, the fate of the Archaic hunters and gatherers becomes an intriguing problem for archaeologists. Did they learn agriculture and settle down like the Anasazi, the prehistoric Pueblo Indians? (For many years, this possibility has been considered a likely one.) Or did they continue their independent life style, taking shelter in temporary huts and lean-tos, moving frequently, hunting small game, and searching out wild plants and seeds? Recent research in the area north of Hovenweep by archaeologists H. W. Toll and William Buckles indicates

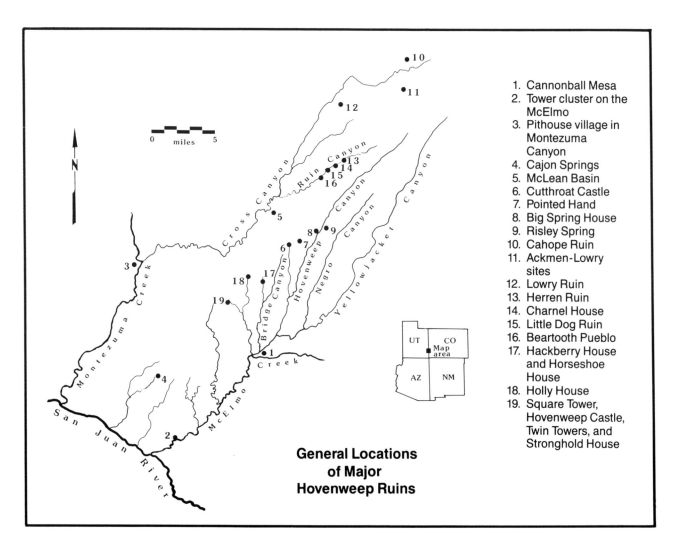

that the Archaic culture survived from the second or third millennium B.C. to historic times. It seems probable, then, that after the Anasazi appeared in the region and built their pueblos and cliff houses, many Archaic groups continued to thrive side by side, as it were, with their new farming neighbors. If this were indeed the case, certain communities probably took on the characteristics of both cultures to varying degrees—hunting, gathering, doing some limited farming, and periodically moving their base camps.

What is particularly fascinating about this notion of a 4,000–5,000 year continuum of an indigenous hunting and gathering culture in the region is that it provides a new perspective on the possible origins of the Ute Indians, who inhabited the area when European explorers first arrived and who still reside on nearby reservations. (The traditional theory concerning Ute origins has been that this tribe expanded into the Mesa Verde region from the southwestern Great Basin after the Anasazi abandoned it in the thirteenth century.) It is exciting to see how ongoing archaeological research at ancient Archaic sites may lead to a new understanding of the history of a living Native American group of people.

THE ANASAZI AT HOVENWEEP

The earliest group of Anasazi Indians in the Four Corners region were people who combined small-scale farming with hunting and foraging. They lived in settled villages, built pithouses for homes, and displayed remarkable expertise in basket weaving: hence their name, Basketmakers. From A.D. 1–500, very few Basketmaker people occupied the Hovenweep area, although a considerable population resided to the east near present-day Durango, and to the west on Cedar Mesa. After this time, more Basketmakers did settle Hovenweep as evidenced by several dozen village and other sites found by archaeologists in areas with deep soil or with good foraging potential. Following A.D. 750, Hovenweep saw a tripling of Basketmaker hamlets, some of which appear to have been fortified or built in defensive locations. As the Basketmaker population grew, were they competing with each other or with an indigenous population for limited food and water resources? More research needs to be done before this question can be resolved.

The number of sites on Cajon Mesa continued to increase after A.D. 900, with Hovenweep and the adjacent Yellowjacket area becoming the northern Anasazi frontier. No doubt this population growth reflected an influx of pioneers from the Dolores region, which was being abandoned. Archaeologists have found Hovenweep sites dating A.D. 900–1150 and ranging from small scatters of stone artifacts to pueblos with many rooms. For the most part, these sites are concentrated on the mesa ridges and surrounding flatland, a condition suggesting that mesa-top dry farming was an important factor in the Hovenweep Anasazi economy of this period. The people were also foraging and using check dams to irrigate small-scale farms in the arroyos. Judging from the large number of sites in all environmental zones and from the lack of defensive characteristics at these sites, one can conclude that the Hovenweep people of this period knew how to use their environment effectively to obtain food.

The Anasazi inhabited Cajon Mesa until A.D. 1300; however, after A.D. 1150, they abandoned many of their mesa-top villages and settlements in favor of large communities established around towers at canyon heads. These graceful towers, which spark the romantic spirits of twentieth-century visitors to Hovenweep National Monument, were associated with massive masonry pueblos, modified springs, rim dams and terraces, and irrigated gardens planted on the talus slopes. Tree-ring dates (a method of dating sites that has made prehistoric southwestern chronology one of the most accurate in the world) indicate that the Anasazi buit their Hovenweep towers between A.D. 1163 and 1277. However, the majority were constructed after A.D. 1230, suggesting that the move to the canyon heads occurred near the end of the period in which the Anasazi lived on Cajon Mesa.

One may wonder why the Hovenweep people moved to the heads of canyons? Perhaps drought made mesa-top farming too unproductive to sustain their numbers, so that they were forced to utilize the permanent springs in the canyons for irrigation. Most likely, the move involved changes in social organization, and probably each of the tower and pueblo complexes formed the center of a farming community based on a variety of water control practices. Whether each community was formed by a localized kin group, such as a group of extended families, is unknown, but it is possible that a descent system of some sort was part of their social organization.

The attempt by the Hovenweep Anasazi to control spring water in the canyons and flood waters rushing over the rims and down the talus slopes apparently succeeded for fifty to a hundred years. The check dam terraces and slick rock reservoirs in the drainages above the towers may have been especially important during this period, particularly if dry farming was impossible. Flood water farming of corn, squash, and beans on the canyon bottoms was also probably practiced, as indicated by the discovery of granaries, storage shelters, hamlets, and corn pollen on flood plains located down canyon from towers. It may also be significant that the canyon heads and talus slopes support the greatest diversity and quantity of small animal and plant life; these resources would have been extremely appealing to a group of people having difficulty subsisting. It also appears that the Hovenweep Anasazi actively encouraged the growth of native edible plants around their garden plots. These would have included beeweed, ground cherry, sedges, milkweed, cattail, and wolf berry.

At Hovenweep, a complex interplay of human history and natural environment must have occurred around the pueblos and the graceful towers. Although the culture ultimately collapsed shortly before A.D. 1300 (just as the Dolores system had collapsed several hundred years earlier), the Hovenweep Anasazi successfully developed a complex agricultural system based on water control technology. Their engineering and architectural traditions produced some of the most beautiful structures in the New World, and they developed a calendrical system equal to that of the Chaco Canyon Anasazi. The three technologies of irrigation, architecture, and calendar were inexorably connected in a socioeconomic system based on agriculture.

THE HOVENWEEP TOWERS

The Hovenweep towers have fascinated explorers and archaeologists since the days of William Henry Jackson, W. H. Holmes, and the Wetherill brothers of the nineteenth century. Even today, on Cajon Mesa hundreds of one-, two-, and three-story towers in various stages of decay grace the banks of springs in the canyon heads and stand on the mesa tops; their locations and intrinsic beauty have generated considerable speculation

Square Tower. Photo by David Noble.

concerning their origin and ancient functions. Circular, square, and D-shaped, the towers were the architectural culmination of a local building tradition that had developed on the ridge tops one to three centuries earlier. Why did this unusual building design evolve? Defense has most often been suggested as the purpose of the towers, for with few, if any, doors or windows, they present a fortified, impregnable appearance. And archaeological evidence does indicate that violence may well have figured into the destruction of certain towers. However, nearly every archaeologist who has worked in the Hovenweep area has offered another speculation regarding the purpose of the towers. Some of these theories have postulated possible uses for food storage, ceremonies, communication, and astronomical observations. Unfortunately, little hard evidence exists to help solve the question, and the speculations are often based on shaky logic, so the topic remains one of Hovenweep's most intriguing mysteries.

During the course of the Hovenweep Project (which I directed between 1974 and 1976), eight towers were investigated, including the earlier mesa-top structures and those at the canyon heads. Although none of the earlier towers revealed clues to indicate their having been used for storage, food preparation, or other economic purposes, a few did have tunnels leading to adjacent kivas. This feature would support a view that at least these particular towers had a ceremonial purpose. In contrast, the canyon head towers constructed later were better built than their predecessors and appear to have served a variety of functions related to agriculture. Every canyon head tower investigated yielded the remains of cultivated crops. Certain towers were grinding rooms, others tool-making or storage areas, and still others kivas. And it appears that some may have been used for calendric purposes. All in all, the wealth of intact ceramic vessels, stone tools, plant remains, and other archaeological features

Hovenweep Castle. Photo by David Noble.

at the towers suggests that a multitude of activities were associated with them. However, all the towers shared their unusual design and striking beauty.

ASTRONOMY AT HOVENWEEP

One function of Hovenweep towers that has received considerable attention in recent years is their possible astronomical or calendric use. Jesse Walter Fewkes first considered this possibility in the early part of the century and more recently Jonathan Reyman, Florence Hawley Ellis, Ray Williamson, and Michael Zeilik have concluded that the movement of light beams cast through tower portholes and doorways upon interior walls could have provided an effective calendar for marking the arrival of the winter and summer solstices and the spring and autumn equinoxes. Because they were farmers, the ability of the Hovenweep Anasazi to anticipate the solstices and equinoxes using

such calendars would have been an extremely important planting and harvesting tool. The calendar was also probably associated with a ceremonial cycle, similar perhaps to that of the present-day Pueblo Indians of New Mexico and Arizona, whose solar calendar is used for both agriculture and ritual purposes.

Four sites at Hovenweep have apparent calendric functions. Of these, three are towers with rectangular sun-watching rooms that have been added onto the original structure. Hovenweep Castle contains probable summer and winter solstice sunset portholes and a possible vernal and autumnal equinox doorway. Unit Type House has sunrise summer and winter solstice as well as equinox portholes and a lunar portal that marks the farthest southern point at which the moon rises. At Cajon Ruins, there are also summer and winter solstice and vernal and autumnal equinox sunset portals.

The most fascinating and dramatic calendric

Solstice sun rays on Holly petroglyph circles. Photo by Joseph Winter.

site at Hovenweep is the petroglyph at Holly ruin, which consists of one concentric circle; two spiral circles; a long, snake-like figure; and a twin-like figure—all of which are pecked into a vertical north-facing slab of rock under an overhang. Because of its orientation, the panel is lit by sunrise light beginning about thirty days before the vernal equinox (March 21), and this lighting effect continues for about thirty days after the autumnal equinox (September 21). As the sun "moves" north and south along the eastern horizon and behind nearby boulders, it casts different configurations of light and shadow on the panel, creating strikingly different patterns at the summer solstice and the equinoxes. At solstice, three separate horizontal rays of light strike all three circles at once, then slowly converge into one bar of light that moves down and over the other elements of the panel. At the equinoxes, the concentric (western) circle is left totally in the dark, while the light beam begins by cutting horizontally across the

Ray of sunlight through tower porthole strikes interior wall where calendrical marker could have been placed. Photo by Joseph Winter.

middle of the center (spiral) circle. It then moves down the panel and cuts the eastern (spiral) circle into an almost perfect third.

The last time I was at Holly was for the 1983 summer solstice sunrise. I had to get there early to find a place, having taken care not to get caught behind the Crow Canyon school bus as it wove and bumped its way along the dirt road, leaving a huge plume of fine choking dust in its wake. After the sunrise show was over, I left Hovenweep and headed back north to my camping spot on Tim Kern's land above Big Spring House. Driving through the pinto bean fields, I realized that in spite of its name, Hovenweep was no longer a "deserted valley." Today, it is frequented by archaeologists, students, and tourists, and inhabited by bean farmers, Park Service rangers, and oil and carbon dioxide field workers. Rumor has it that the roads to Hovenweep National Monument soon will be paved, attracting still more visitors to the towers and seeps among the cottonwoods. Also in progress is the Dolores Project irrigation system, which will change local farming from dry bean fields and winter wheat to totally new crops. Just as the Anasazi farmers of Hovenweep replaced an indigenous hunting and gathering system with acres of cultivated corn, beans, and squash, so too are twentieth-century Hovenweep economic "pioneers" challenging the traditions and life style of the area's long time residents. The Anasazi eventually departed, and no doubt today's generation will someday leave. Who can guess how long it may be before Hovenweep is once again a deserted valley?

Joseph Winter is director of the Office of Contract Archaeology and associate professor of anthropology at the University of New Mexico. From 1974 to 1976, he was director of the Hovenweep Archaeological Project.

CRAFT ARTS of the Mesa Verdeans

By Richard W. Lang

There is a quality of Eden-lost in this space. A sanctity peculiar to high places and their quietudes hangs on the breezes of the Mesa Verde; and in the scale of its narrow, pine-sheltered canyons and small, scattered ruins, modern man finds an unusual intimacy with the past. The Green Mesa draws us to it by these and other qualities, through our sometimes paradoxical veneration of the ancient and by our wonderfully unquench-able curiosity.

In their mysterious, hallowed vacancy, the stone villages whisper un-easily of life's fragility, of those dark bogies of chance and the unpredict-able that haunt our progress and erase our labors and our loves with alarming regularity. In the unadorned, almost stark, beauty of rock and mud transformed by mind and hand, these little towns and farmsteads speak praise for common works and qualitative thought, for the pursuit of art in all our undertakings. Their compact and ordered aspect, their rustic artistry, are true reflections of the lives and attitudes of their builders.

Among the people of the Mesa Verde, knowledge was largely practical and spiritual, and was transmitted with little personal modification over short generations and long centuries. Change came slowly, great changes developing progressively out of earlier, minor ones. Invention and crea-tivity were expressed in subtle ways within a framework of traditional

Classic Black-on-white kiva jar. Courtesy, MVNP. Photo by David Noble.

Hafted hammer. Courtesy, MVNP. Photo by Fred Mang.

Large coiled basket. Courtesy, MVNP. Photo by Fred Mang.

Cloth fragment. Courtesy, MVNP. Photo by Fred Mang.

modes. Art was everywhere, and the most utilitarian of objects was often deftly created with the greatest care.

Care, quality, and a sound understanding of the properties and potentials of the raw materials at hand are written broadly on the artifacts of Mesa Verde. Such aspirations and knowledge remain embodied in the finely flaked knives of gray flint and the carved and polished bone of flesher and awl. These and other tools were made well and made to work. The on-goingness of humankind depended on it. Stone hoes and wooden digging sticks prodded and cut the earth for planting and tending of the all-important crops of corn, beans, and squash. Stone axes bit the tough wood of juniper or the softer wood of pine in the procurement of the stuff from which roof beams or cradles are made. Serviceable coiled, twilled, and plaited baskets of willow, oak, yucca, and rabbitbrush may have held the day's laundry or the meal fresh from the metate. Blankets of cotton, fur, feathers, and twine kept off winter's chill. The list of objects and functions goes on and on, in correspondence with the many needs of a people whose daily existence and survival necessarily centered on the ability of each individual to glean from field and woodland the sustenance that each required. Given the moisture-bearing winter snows, timely rains, and good soil, the Mesa Verdeans were a people self-sufficient in all that was necessary to the good life.

Science and history provide us with the only time-machines that we possess. However, were we to be allowed a day on Mesa Verde in that time when Cliff Palace or Long House echoed the voices of their inhabitants, our minds would be boggled by the range and depth of knowledge of simple things held by each of those inhabitants. To them, a field of cactus, yucca and grasses was not a barren place, but a storehouse and a garden that would, with the passing of seasons, yield fiber for cordage, footwear, baskets, and more, as well as fruits, seeds, tubers, and dyes. A graceful and magnificent buck mule deer was far more than a fellow creature to be admired from the roadside. He was a source of much needed protein, hide, sinew, oil, bone, and antler. From the body of that deer came human energy, stitching materials, the tools of the weaver and tanner, shoes, shirts, and blankets, and the hard tine used to flake the flint.

Of all that the Mesa Verdean's have left in their passing, the most impressive is certainly their architecture, but perhaps the most appealing is their pottery. For the modern Pueblos and, presumably, for their Anasazi predecessors, both clay and the knowledge of pottery making were gifts from the gods, who enjoined them never to forget this skill so important to their well-being.

The fundamental techniques of the potter's art first filtered into the Southwest from Mexico around 300 B.C. Gradually over the following eight-hundred years these techniques diffused to most of the peoples of the southwestern culture area. The idea of pottery making did not come to these northern peoples as an isolated trait, but rather as part of a developed Mexican complex, which included agriculture, domestic turkeys, and the concepts and elements of settled village life. Within the mobile life style of earlier southwestern hunter-gatherers, there would have existed no real basis for either use or desire for the rather fragile tool that is pottery. However, during the last millennium of the years B.C., the northern bands began to experiment with rudimentary farming, working it into the fabric of their cultures, and generation to generation saw agriculture change their lives. Farming both required and facilitated a more sedentary life style, just as the processing of corn led to the modification of old tools and the adoption of new ones, such as ceramics.

When this pottery craft appeared in the Mesa Verde, it was full-blown and formed part of the cultural baggage of farmers settling the Colorado highlands in the late A.D. 500s. The pottery that these early settlers brought with them from the valleys of the San Juan River drainage was in most ways typical of that found among their Anasazi brethren scattered across the northern Southwest in hundreds of unimposing pit-house villages. It was a gray ware, open fired without free access of oxygen, so that carbonaceous matter in the clay remained unburned. The result is pottery of gray color, which is emblematic of most Anasazi ceramics.

The clay used in the Mesa Verde region may have been mined from the Mancos Shale, deposited by a stagnant sea that had slowly advanced over southwestern Colorado more than sixty-five million years before. To counteract shrinkage of the vessel walls and lessen the risk of cracking during the drying and firing process, the clay was tempered with minute fragments of even older igneous rock, formed when the crust of the planet was first in the making. Mixed with water, these vestiges of a poisonous, firey Earth and ancient oceans, were transformed into malleable ropes of tempered clay, coiled concentrically, then pressed, pulled, scraped, and rubbed into desired shapes. And shapes there were many: pitchers and bowls, small, globe-shaped, neckless jars and large ones with long, slender necks; canteens, dippers, and ladles patterned after the familiar gourd vessels unembellished or adorned with lugs and handles for holding and hanging. These varied forms reflect the range of needs for storage, transport, cooking, and service—all the many everyday tasks that pottery facilitated.

Most vessels were left undecorated, but some were painted with a red, earthy wash and others with simple, appealing geometrics, suggestive of basketry designs, fired black to reddish-brown against the open, gray field of the container's surface. For these, iron-bearing mineral paints or carbon-based paints made from plant extracts were used.

Over the next seven hundred years many changes occurred in Mesa Verde pottery. Between A.D. 700 and 1000, oxidized, red-fired pottery saw some use, and red washes went out of style. Corrugations, formed of unobliterated coils, appeared as a decorative zone on the necks of jars by the late 700s, and by the 1000s, such corrugations often covered the entire exterior surface of storage and cooking jars with wide, belled mouths. The corrugations were manipulated for decorative effect in a number of ways, the most common of which was uniform indenting with the fingertip to provide a crimped effect. This extensive exterior texturing made these jars easier to grip and may have had other functions as well. With time, polishing of painted surfaces became more common, and painted designs more elaborate and complex. Although local and individual variation in forms, surface finish, and design are apparent, many of the changes seen in Mesa Verde pottery over its long span reflect broad shifts in function and style that periodically swept across the Anasazi world. Many of these seem to have been of ultimate Mexican origin, while others mark southwestern innovations. Both passed on from one group to another through trade and other contacts. The potters of each region drew selectively from these idea pools, not only adopting but adapting forms, motifs, and complexes of design in a manner distinctive to their own people.

Many of the ceramic works of the Mesa Verdeans of the Pueblo II and III periods of about 900 to 1300 are true masterpieces in clay. While some contemporary Pueblo potters have attempted revival of indented-corrugated pottery, none has yet achieved the fineness of surface texturing

Corrugated jar with spiral decoration. Courtesy, MVNP. Photo by Fred Mang.

Jar with flattened corrugations and indented spiral band. Courtesy, MVNP. Photo by Fred Mang.

Mancos black-on-white bowl. Courtesy MVNP. Photo by David Noble.

Ceramic bowl. Collections, School of American Research. Photo by Lynn Lown.

Black-on-white pitcher. Courtesy, MVNP. Photo by Fred Mang.

or the thinness of wall regularly seen in this prehistoric gray ware. But, without doubt, the highest ceramic accomplishments of the Mesa Verde potter are found in a black-painted, white-slipped pottery termed *Mesa Verde Black-on-white*.

Pueblo potters have traditionally given "life" to their pots through their own breath, and in the strength and beauty of Mesa Verde Black-on-white that life clearly lingers. The designs and finish of this pottery exhibit a bold perfection. Even in vessel wall thickness and the density of white to gray slips, there is an implication of delicate solidity. There is a strong balance of light and dark in the largely abstract, geometric designs arranged with a high consciousness of symmetry. In looking at this pottery, one cannot help but suspect that the potters of the thirteenth

Black-on-white mugs. Clifford Chappel collection at the Anasazi Heritage Center. Photo by Alden Hayes. Courtesy, MVNP.

Black-on-white ceramic jar. Courtesy, MVNP. Photo by Fred Mang.

century lived in a tightly organized society, and further, that they saw the decorating of ceramics as one of its high arts. Long gone are the truly whimsical qualities that characterized much earlier design and which continued into the 1100s. Here, structure and detail are paramount.

Rarely do we see biomorphic forms incorporated into the design of Mesa Verde pottery, but they do occur. Among them are wonderfully stylized representations of the macaw, the sacred bird of the Sun; a racing herd of deer or sheep; a dancing hermaphrodite; a flock of feeding ducks, entranced, awaiting the arrows of a supernatural hunter; a dancer, half man, half bighorn sheep, leaping across the exterior of a painted bowl; and the ubiquitous Humpback, playing out the tune of life upon his flute, urging, Pan-like, increase of man, plant, and beast.

Kokopelli figure on a Mesa Verde Black-on-white bowl. Courtesy Edgar Gilliland. Photo by David Noble.

Ceramic ladle. Collections, School of American Research. Photo by Lynn Lown.

Black-on-white bowl with bird figures. Courtesy, MVNP. Photo by Fred Mang.

Fragments from black-on-white bowl. Courtesy, MVNP. Photo by Fred Mang.

Carved stone lion effigy. Courtesy, MVNP. Photo by J. W. Fewkes.

These depictions are tangible expressions of a society in which human action is central to the course of natural events, in which all is bound by a shared understanding of life and its ultimate purpose, by the linkages of man, nature, and spirit. Even the hunter and the ducks possess a shared view of rightness in the world of the Mesa Verde towns, communities that sustained the moral order in which the guiding focus of everyday activities was continuity, balance, and fecundity in all things. Here religion had the power to call the deer and draw goodness from an invisible world that was everywhere, that literally invested art with spirit and gave life to the very stones.

In the surviving arts and crafts of Mesa Verde, we are privileged to have contact with one of many adaptations that triumphed for a little while on the timeline of human experiment. Through these remains, we find appreciation for the Mesa Verdean accomplishment, for its creative simplicity and down-to-earth practicalities. Certainly theirs was a far from perfect society. Life made hard demands on these people. Old age came quickly, and children and adults often encountered death prematurely. Food was not always plentiful and the harsh environment was ultimately unforgiving. It is also safe to guess that it was a culture of relatively narrow vision, in which the social bond overrode reason, and both reason and action existed largely within a sometimes uncompromising traditional and corporate structure. Nonetheless, there are aspects of this culture that are worthy of our contemplation, that can perhaps speak to us in useful ways about our dwindling self-reliance; our voids in understanding of place and environment; about human-centered processes in which technology and organization serve the concrete needs of people, rather than vice versa; about the virtues of quality, community, smallness, and simplicity. Perhaps among the ashes, sherds, and crumbling walls, we may find a strange and unexpected sort of wisdom.

Richard W. Lang is director of the Wheelwright Museum of the American Indian in Santa Fe and a former staff member of the School of American Research. He is an anthropologist and artist and the author of numerous works on the archaeology and native cultures of the Southwest.

Why Did They Leave and Where Did They Go?

By Linda S. Cordell

I first visited the ruins of Mesa Verde as an archaeology student, during a mid-season break in fieldwork at the Sapawe site near El Rito, New Mexico. There were few trees at Sapawe, and I had become accustomed to the hot, dusty, barren landscape. It seemed as though when we crossed the state line into Colorado, the environment at once became cool, green, and inviting. Mesa Verde

was lush with piñon, juniper, and dense underbrush. Looking at the shaded ruins and the wonderful green canyons beneath the cliff dwellings, I could not imagine why the Anasazi had left. Not until a few years later, while still a student, did I very carefully read and think about the various explanations archaeologists had advanced to account for the puzzle of abandonment at Mesa Verde.

The Anasazi occupied Mesa Verde for some 800 years, from about A.D. 500 to 1300. Throughout most of that time, their numbers apparently increased. Most archaeologists suggest, on the basis of the numbers of probably occupied rooms, that the highest population in the area—perhaps 2,500 people —was attained sometime between about 1150 and 1250. Tree-ring dates indicate that the last construction took place in the late 1270s, and that by 1300, the Anasazi had permanently abandoned the mesa.

Two factors warrant mention before reviewing the traditional reasons given for people abandoning their homes or towns (*abandonment*). First, while good ideas are easily generated, scientific substantiation of them is difficult. The real challenge of archaeology lies in developing methods to evaluate and judge ideas about the past. Second, most reasons for abandonments have been presented as *the* single cause, as though a file containing all the articles attempting to piece together the puzzle of abandonment could be stamped SOLVED and put away forever. But abandonments—including the one that occurred at Mesa Verde—are complex events or processes, and it is most likely that they involve a combination of factors.

TRADITIONAL EXPLANATIONS FOR ABANDONMENT

The devastating effect of a major drought was one of the earliest explanations offered for the desertion of Mesa Verde. The drought hypothesis received support in 1929, when A. E. Douglass demonstrated his new technique of tree-ring dating, culminating in that year with his development of a sequence of past annual tree-ring widths covering more than a thousand years (an achievement that marked the beginning of dendroclimatology). The tree-rings showed a period of severe drought between A.D. 1276 and 1299 on the Colorado Plateau.

While the occurrence of this drought has gone unchallenged, some researchers have questioned its relationship to regional abandonments, particularly since some famous sites, such as Betatakin and Kiet Siel in northeastern Arizona were built at precisely the time when they should have been abandoned if the drought were of regional importance. And Hopi villages that are in settings generally much more arid than Mesa Verde were occupied throughout the so-called Great Drought. In fact, the complete tree-ring sequence from Mesa Verde shows a number of very severe droughts before the one between 1276 and 1299; yet during these, Mesa Verde Anasazi knew how to cope with the drought problem. Or was the final drought the last straw?

A suggestion similar to the Great Drought hypothesis is that arroyo cutting drastically decreased the amount of farmland. Either drought conditions or prehistoric cutting of timber for building material, firewood, and the clearing of agricultural fields or a combination of both factors could have begun such a cycle of severe erosion. The loss of fields due to gullying has had harmful effects on Hopi farms in the twentieth century, and such a phenomenon might have been a major problem in the prehistoric past. But did it cause abandonment? Archaeological surveys of Wetherill and Chapin mesas at Mesa Verde have recorded hundreds of stone check dams that the Anasazi built across arroyos. Since these dams are still effectively preventing erosion today, the Anasazi seem to have solved the problem quite well.

Abandonment has also been frequently attributed to warfare either with "hostile nomads" or with other Anasazi. Harold S. Gladwin provides one of my favorite warfare quotes. In *A History of the Ancient Southwest* (The Bond Wheelwright Company, 1957), he wrote, "In every village in the Southwest at A.D. 1200, the same questions are being asked: Where to go? What to do? to obtain relief from the ceaseless persecution of marauding Athabascans," (p. 269). Despite the colorful phrasing, the existence of such an Athapaskan menace does not appear at all

Arroyo cutting

likely. First, the Athapaskans, who were the ancestors of the modern Navajos and Apaches, entered the Southwest nearly 200 years after Mesa Verde was abandoned. Second, before Europeans introduced the horse, nomads, whether Athapaskan or not, would not have been much of a threat to the Anasazi villages. Without the ability to carry out swift surprise attacks on horseback, small bands of hunters and gatherers would have been at an extreme tactical disadvantage in confronting a fortified pueblo.

Other anthropologists have argued that the peaceful nature of Pueblo Indians is much exaggerated, and that in any case it is the result of their subjugation by Europeans for the past 300 years. Perhaps then, abandonment was the result of warfare or aggression among the Pueblos themselves? Certainly no society is either inherently peaceful or aggressive and warlike. Yet, physical evidence of conflict, such as burned villages or skeletons with mortal wounds, is lacking. A few years ago, one of my graduate students, much enamoured with the ideas of the defensive nature of some Anasazi sites and the role of prehistoric hostilities in abandonment, pursued the topic of warfare for a term paper. Much to our enlightenment—but to his chagrin—he found that the only strong pattern in the literature was one linking the modern publication dates of articles supporting the warfare hypothesis with times when the United States was just about to enter a major war, or was fighting one. The aggression model seems to tell us more about ourselves than about the Anasazi!

The tragic factional dispute that culminated in the split and near desertion of the Hopi village of Oraibi in 1906 suggested to some that factionalism might have been the root of the prehistoric abandonments as well. Critics of this explanation point out that the conflict at Oraibi was largely the result of U.S. Government intervention in the Hopi way of life; and, thus, they argue it is not an appropriate model for the prehistoric period. Unfortunately, factionalism is common among villagers throughout the world, and sometimes does lead to the breaking up of communities. However, as at the Hopi Third Mesa, after such disputes new villages are generally founded in the immediate vicinity. Thus, historic and sociological evidence indicates that the hypothesis of unresolvable factional disputes can-

not explain the abandonment of the entire Mesa Verde region.

Densely inhabited villages and poor sanitary practices leading to epidemic disease have also been cited as causes of abandonment. There is little evidence to substantiate or refute this idea. Large burial populations are lacking, contrary to expectation if the idea were true. Available skeletal remains sometimes show evidence indicating poor nutrition; however, the infectious diseases that cause epidemics generally do not leave observable marks on skeletons, so the remains provide no proof of the occurrence of epidemics.

Finally, it has been suggested that poor nutrition and declining birth rates may have greatly reduced the population and caused the saddened and discouraged survivors to leave. Porotic hyperostosis, which is a skeletal condition in which the bone is visibly pitted or spongy looking, is found on Mesa Verde skeletons and has been viewed as evidence of poor nutrition and anemia. Yet even this evidence is ambiguous. Modern clinical studies indicate that many conditions, such as short but severe childhood illness, may cause porotic hyperostosis, and that these conditions may not relate to the general health status of the population.

Drought, arroyo cutting, warfare, factionalism, and disease are the most common reasons cited for abandonment. None has gone unquestioned as the single cause. More likely, a combination of factors, including some of those traditionally given, was responsible.

NEW VIEWS ON THE ABANDONMENT QUESTION

During the past four or five years, some southwestern archaeologists have begun to explore the abandonment issue from a different perspective. Rather than searching for a single cause, they consider

Malnutrition

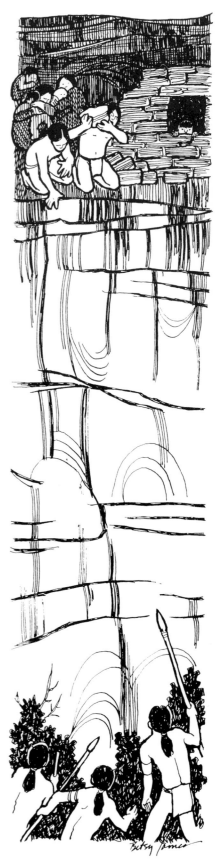

Hostilities

37

questions about the Anasazi in light of knowledge about ancient and modern agriculturists worldwide. Their approach also takes into consideration new, highly refined, and precise information about the past climate of the Colorado Plateau.

In our own society, we are accustomed to settlement stability. Boston and New York have not become ghost towns despite the growth of Los Angeles and San Diego. Paris, London, and Rome have much longer histories. In the Near East, the landscape is dotted with *tells* representing the accumulations of millenniums. Yet, in most of the Western Hemisphere before European contact, the abandonment of centers of population was relatively common. The Maya centers of Tikal and Chichen Itza, the Oaxacan center of Monte Alban, the Mississippian sites of Cahokia in East St. Louis, Kincaid and Angel on the lower Ohio River, and Moundville in Alabama, as well as thousands of other sites, were all abandoned before Europeans ventured to the Americas. While none of these examples is directly analogous to Mesa Verde, there are some parallels. For example, virtually all of the lowland Maya centers were abandoned prehistorically. (It is interesting that single settlements in the Americas were rarely occupied for as long as single settlements in the Near East or Europe. In this context, perhaps the stability of settlements is the mystery requiring explanation.)

Tree-ring studies indicate that even the largest southwestern sites were rarely occupied for more than about eighty years, and smaller sites for much shorter periods of time. As long as land was plentiful, it appears that the Anasazi met problems arising from local depletion of resources, such as firewood, by simply moving on. In historic times, Pueblo Indians are known to have traveled nearly 200 miles to hunt or to gather seasonal resources such as piñon nuts. However, when resources are needed daily, as wood is for cooking and heating, long distance expeditions may become a greater burden than simply moving to a new location.

Epidemics

There is also a common pattern in prehistoric southwestern occupations: the inhabitants of a region would occupy and then abandon a locality, such as a single stream valley or mesa, one or more times. Such cases rarely are mysterious; the people seem to have moved to neighboring areas, often because minor climatic changes necessitated short distance moves to slightly higher or lower elevations where growing conditions were better for crops.

Prehistoric abandonments of larger regions—such as the Mesa Verde/northern San Juan River drainage, Chaco Canyon and the San Juan Basin, the Mogollon Mountains, and the central Gila and Salt drainages—are somewhat more complex, however. They are not necessarily the result of an accumulation of smaller residential moves, nor were all of these large areas abandoned at the same time. Had such simultaneous abandonments occurred, they might suggest a pan-southwestern event of major proportions. In each case, abandonment followed a period of population growth accompanied by a breakdown of older regional trade ties and the replacement of formal, planned village layouts by more casual architectural arrangements. In the Mesa Verde and San Juan Basin areas, tree-ring studies suggest that the social disruption coincided with a period of less predictable rainfall.

These observations indicate that the eventual abandonment of villages in the Mesa Verde region may reflect the inability of the social system to sustain dense populations. This condition may have existed in part because an unpredictable rainfall pattern did not allow sufficient food surplus to be stored against poor crop years. In any case, as the older settlements were abandoned, new and very large communities were founded in regions that had previously been only sparsely inhabited. The new centers along the Chama and Rio Grande valleys, on the Zuni Plateau, and in the Upper Little Colorado area established new trade networks and gradually attracted population from surrounding areas. Although Mesa Verde and other formerly central settlements were no longer centers of village life, they may well have continued to be used as places where people gathered wild food and perhaps occasionally farmed.

WHICH WAY DID THEY GO?

During the fourteenth century, very large villages were founded along the Chama River, central and northern Rio Grande, Rio Puerco (east), upper Pecos River, and their tributaries, as well as westward in central western New Mexico and central Arizona. These villages were almost certainly founded by a combination of migrants from abandoned areas and long-time local residents. Many of these villages are considered ancestral sites by the modern Pueblo Indians of New

Factionalism

Mexico and Arizona. For example, Puye is considered the ancestral village of modern Santa Clara Pueblo. Atsinna and Hawikku are among the ancestral Zuni villages, and the Homolovi ruins and Chavez Pass Pueblo are ancestral Hopi sites. There is little question that among the modern Pueblo Indians are the descendants of the vanished people of Mesa Verde.

There are, however, issues that can involve hours of debate over countless cups of coffee: such discussions are concerned with defining the route each migrant group took and which of the modern Pueblo village groups are direct descendants of the people from Mesa Verde (or Chaco Canyon, Canyon de Chelly, the Flagstaff area, or other locations). There is no consensus now nor, I believe, will there ever be. The key issue is that there exists no neat string of sites built in Mesa Verde style, for example, nor does a trail of Mesa-Verde-style ceramics lead from the mesa to a particular group of currently inhabited or ancestral villages. If one starts with the present and works backward, sifting through the migration legends extant among all the Pueblos, there is again no direct route or link. And so the endless scholarly arguments continue.

Actually, we know from countless ethnographic examples, including those of the Pueblo Indians, that when villages are abandoned, the people do not move as a single group. The most frequent pattern is that individuals and family groups follow separate migration paths and integrate themselves into ongoing communities with which they have kinship or friendship ties.

To archaeologists, this form of migration would be visible primarily as an increase of the population in certain regions, which is precisely what we see. This form of migration also closely fits the complex pattern of village splitting and reorganization that is common to the migration legends.

DISCUSSION

Abandonment and migrations linking ancient Anasazi sites to the modern Pueblo villages have been themes in the exploration of southwestern prehistory for more than 100 years. The more archaeologists learn about Anasazi society and the past climate of the Southwest, the more complex the issues of abandonment and migration become. The abandonment of Mesa Verde nearly 700 years ago was probably due to a combination of

factors: more variation in summer rainfall than had occurred in the past, depletion of wood supplies for heating and building material, and failure of the social ties of trade and exchange to provide for the people's needs. With life in general becoming more difficult, factional disputes likely broke out more often, and some people sought more peaceful new homes with relatives and friends at distant villages. Possibly, too, disputes between villages occurred over access to farmland or firewood, and again some of the people may have left to seek their fortunes elsewhere.

After not too many years, the new villages in the Upper Rio Grande drainage and in the Upper Little Colorado River and the Zuni areas became large settlements— active centers of social and religious life and important links in new networks of trade and exchange. As such, they may have been very attractive destinations for the migrants.

Over the past twenty years, I have returned to Mesa Verde several times. On each visit I am again impressed with how green and cool and lovely it is. When I think only of the landscape, the abandonment seems a great mystery. But then I wonder how it would have felt to remain among those who watched their friends and children leave, knowing that now there would be fewer people to help with the daily work, fewer visitors bringing trade goods and news, and not enough people to hold the important ceremonies that marked the passage of the seasons. My guess is that, weighed against human fellowship and a rich and secure social life, the quiet canyons and mesas would lose every time.

Linda Cordell is an archaeologist and professor of anthropology at the University of New Mexico. She is the author of Prehistory of the Southwest *(1984, Academic Press).*

Other titles on the National Parks of the Southwest:

Houses Beneath the Rock: the Anasazi of Canyon de Chelly and Navajo National Monument, edited by David Grant Noble

Pecos Ruins: Geology, Archaeology, History and Prehistory, edited by David Grant Noble

Zuni and El Moro: Past and Present, edited by David Grant Noble

Salinas: Archaeology, History and Prehistory, edited by David Grant Noble

Wupatki and Walnut Canyon: New Perspectives on History, Prehistory and Rock Art, edited by David Grant Noble

The Magic of Bandelier, by David E. Stuart

For further information on current pricing and shipping, please contact:

Ancient City Press
P.O. Box 5401
Santa Fe, New Mexico 87502
(505) 982-8195